Hand Appliqué

with Alex Anderson

SEVEN PROJECTS FOR HAND APPLIQUÉ

C&T PUBLISHING

2001 © Alex Anderson
Illustrations and How-to Photography 2001 © C&T Publishing, Inc.

Developmental Editor:	Liz Aneloski
Technical Editor:	Joyce Engels Lytle
Copy Editor:	Carol Barrett
Design Director:	Diane Pedersen
Production Assistant:	Kirstie L. McCormick
Book Designer:	Rose Sheifer
Cover Designer:	Christina Jarumay
Illustrator:	Lee Nelson
Quilt Photographer:	Sharon Risedorph
Cover Photographer:	Chris Burke

Published by C&T Publishing, Inc., P.O. Box 1456, Lafayette, California 94549

Attention Teachers:
C&T Publishing, Inc. encourages you to use this book as a text for teaching. Contact us at 800-284-1114 or www.ctpub.com for more information about the C&T Teachers Program.

Trademarked (™) and Registered Trademarked (®) names are used throughout this book. Rather than use the symbols with every occurrence of a trademark and registered trademark name, we are using the names only in an editorial fashion and to the benefit of the owner, with no intention of infringement.

Library of Congress Cataloging-in-Publication Data
Anderson, Alex
  Hand appliqué with Alex Anderson : seven projects for hand appliqué.
     p. cm.
  ISBN 1-57120-151-3
  1. Appliqué--Patterns. 2. Quilts. I. Title.
  TT779 .A525 2001
  746.46'041--dc21   00-011629

Printed in Singapore

10 9 8 7 6 5 4 3 2 1

CONTENTS

Acknowledgments

Through all of your kind spirits and willingness to help me, you, my friends, made this book possible. A special thank you to

Robert Callaham, whose appliqué is perfection. Your kind spirit and helpful advice helped make this book a reality.

Nancy Sands, whose fine hand helped complete many of the projects.

Paula Reid, who didn't complain about brutal quilting deadlines.

Introduction

I love appliqué. What appliqué offers to the quiltmaking world cannot be matched in any other format. By layering shapes of fabric on top of background fabrics you can create numerous designs and patterns that are difficult, if not impossible, to achieve with piecing. If you have never tried this form of quiltmaking, now is the time. Whether your quilt is crying out for a border graced with leaves and flowers or a simple wallhanging is on your agenda, it's time to overcome any fears and put your fabric, needle, thread, and thimble to work!

The great thing about appliqué is that there isn't just one way to accomplish your project. One quilter might share her favorite approach with you, while another will boast a different technique as her favorite. There are several ways to approach appliqué, each with its own benefits. The great news is that you get to choose what works best for you! Each technique offers opportunities to handle different appliqué situations. In this book I will share what I have found to be useful for basic appliqué. When you become comfortable with the different elements of appliqué, you will be free to explore the endless possibilities. Baltimore album, Jacobean style, and storybook quilts are just the beginning once a basic foundation has been laid. Now, it's time to get to work! Before you know it, you will love appliqué as much as I do!

Supplies

Fabric

It is important to work with the best 100% cotton fabrics available—typically found at your local quilt shop. It is important to understand that the quality of 100% cotton fabric varies. Some of the cotton fabrics available to us are printed on greige goods with a lesser thread count and improper processing. This fabric can be difficult to work with because it can fray excessively and can be difficult to needle turn. When your quilt is finished, the dyes might run or the fabric might pucker when you wash it. A lot of time goes into appliqué, so don't sacrifice your results with a poor quality fabric.

The background fabric will set the mood of your quilt. Is your quilt bright and cheery, like *Cherries* on page 30, or dramatic and rich like *Autumn Leaves* on page 27? Another option is to piece your background like *Rail Fence with Stars* on page 36. This gives another element to the appliqué blocks. Just make sure that your background provides a strong contrast of value (light and dark) for the shapes you are going to appliqué on top. If not, your quilt will lack the pizzazz we quilters love.

It's fun to choose the fabrics for the appliquéd shapes. Typically, appliqué motifs are recognizable designs, so I try to find fabrics that portray the subject matter. For instance, if I am creating cherries, I look for several reds that represent the subtle variety of colors of cherries. Tone-on-tone and sparkle fabrics work very well. Tone-on-tone fabrics are typically monochromatic (all one color) and subtly solid, but there is enough interest in the print that it helps hide less-than-perfect stitches. Sparkle fabrics (those that include a color/colors that are light or bright to add sparkle to the quilt) are also monochromatic, but in addition have a complete range of value (light to dark). They are a little trickier to work with, but you can achieve interesting results, like the effect of the sun sparkling on the bright red skin of a cherry. The subtle color variations in hand-dyed fabrics are also wonderful for appliqué. My only word of caution is to make sure that you test for colorfastness or prewash to remove the excess dye. If the dye continues to run, I would pass on that piece of fabric no matter how much it cost.

For your first appliqué endeavor, stay away from solid-colored fabrics since the stitches will show more. Save that challenge for after you perfect the stitch. Also, it is generally best to avoid fabrics that are printed with large-scale designs. A lot of subtleties are possible with appliqué, and they can be missed if the fabric is highly patterned.

One of the many great things about appliqué is that you can cut and audition your fabric shapes on the background until you are happy with the effect. This leaves a lot of room for creativity and makes last minute changes possible.

Equipment

Needles

There are several types of needles to choose from, each with its own benefits. I would start with size 11 sharps needles. They are long, slender, and easy to work with. Some people prefer a betweens needle. Betweens are smaller than most people are used to and are specifically designed for hand quilting. However, if you are adept at hand quilting, you might like the feel of the smaller needle. Another option is straw or milliner's needles; they are longer than sharps. These needles are a little harder to find, but if you like the feel of the sharps you might want to try straw or milliner needles to see if you like either of them. One last consideration is the size of the eye of the needle. Is it large enough to thread without difficulty? Getting started should be a joy, not an agonizing experience.

Thread

Thread is an important issue with appliqué. First and foremost your thread should match the color of the appliqué piece, not the background. At first this might seem like a costly investment as you look at all the colors in your quilt, but before too long you will have a complete range of colors that will last you a long time. Just like needles, there are different threads you can try. The most common thread is the 50 weight, 100% cotton thread you probably use on your sewing machine. This thread will work fine. However, there are finer threads available that will help hide your stitches. One type of thread is made for machine embroidery; it is 60 weight. It costs about the same as sewing machine thread and is available in a variety of colors. Silk thread is wonderful to work with—it hides the stitches even more than the machine embroidery thread, but it is costly. If you decide to indulge and use silk thread, all you really need to purchase are a light taupe, dark gray, and few primary colors. Silk thread is adept at hiding in the cloth; so it is not mandatory to purchase a complete range of colors. Embroidery floss and perle (pearl) cotton thread both work well for buttonhole appliqué. Like fabric, you shouldn't skimp on thread quality. Working with quality products will pay off immensely in the short and long run.

Thimbles

A thimble is used to help push the needle through the layers of fabric. Unlike hand quilting, a thimble is not required for appliqué. However, if the appliqué bug bites you, a thimble will become a treasured tool, since the needle will start to wear holes in your pushing finger. The thimble should fit snugly enough so it will not fall off when you gently shake your hand.

Scissors

You will need three pairs of scissors: one for fabric, one for thread and intricate cutting, and one for paper. Your thread and fabric scissors should be of excellent quality with a sharp point and small enough to handle easily. Hide these from your family—they should be kept as good as new for best results.

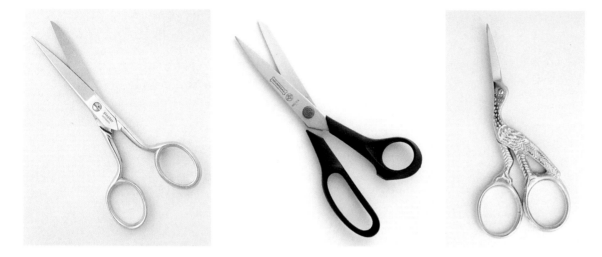

Pins

Use good pins. The large, bargain-brand quilting pins are not appropriate. Because of their size they will get in the way and be worth more trouble than the money they saved you. Typically the smaller the length of the pins the better. Some people like the tiny sequin pins available from craft stores. I like the extra-fine 1⅜" 0.50 mm, glass-head pins I use for machine piecing.

Template Materials

Template Plastic

When cutting multiple copies of the same shape it's good to have a sturdy pattern to trace around. Lightweight cardboard or card stock will work, but paper products will eventually become soft and bend at the edges after multiple tracings. Ideally, I like to use translucent template plastic available at your local quilt shop. There are several different brands to choose from, both light and heavyweight. The lightweight material (or x-ray film) will work fine for tracing shapes, but for circles you need to purchase the heavyweight, heat-resistant plastic Templar or pre-cut circles created for this purpose.

Freezer Paper

That's right, freezer paper, the kind grandma used! Freezer paper is coated on one side with plastic that sticks to your fabric when pressed with a very hot dry iron. You can purchase freezer paper on a roll at your local grocery store.

Bias Bars

Bias bars are long, flat sticks in various widths designed specifically for making stems. They are available either in metal or coated-metal—both are heat resistant. The metal bars give a good, sharp, clean shape when pressed, but can burn you if you aren't careful when pressing the fabric into position because they aren't as heat-resistant as the coated-metal bars. The coated-metal bars don't get as hot, but because of this heat-resistant coating, these bars are thicker so it is difficult to get a nice flat edge.

Marking Tools

There are several different marking tools available. For appliqué I like the General's Charcoal White® pencil available at quilt and art supply stores. It allows you to mark a good line and rubs off easily. For light-colored fabrics I use an extra-hard lead mechanical pencil. Always test the marking tool on the fabric you intend to use to make sure it will eventually rub or wash off. Strange and unfortunate things have been known to happen even with the best of products.

Miscellaneous Supplies

Other general supplies needed are a good, hot iron, sewing machine, spray starch, rotary cutting tools, comfortable chair, good light, and possibly magnifying glasses from your local drug store (for the over 40-year-old crowd).

Optional

- Water soluble glue stick
- Lightweight fusible web
- Lap desk

General Instructions

Grain

Understanding the grain of fabric is very important in quiltmaking. When fabric is produced the threads are woven in two directions. The two long finished edges of the fabric are called the selvages. For piecing or appliqué, it is always best to cut off the selvages. For appliqué the selvage is thick and difficult to stitch through. For piecing, the selvage can pucker and cause distortion. The length of the fabric is called the lengthwise grain, and it has the least amount of stretch. The width of the fabric is called the crosswise grain, and it has a little more stretch. The length and crosswise grain are considered the straight of grain. The diagonal crossgrain is called the bias, and it has a lot of stretch. When deciding how to position your appliqué patterns on the fabric to be cut out, place the curves of the shape on the bias whenever possible. This will help create smooth, curved edges.

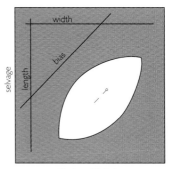

Grain of Fabric

Pressing

While pressing may seem like an insignificant part of quiltmaking, it alone can determine the success of a quilt. Always press the fabric before cutting into it. Working with rumpled fabric will guarantee unsatisfactory results.

When pressing for appliqué, I approach the process very differently than for piecing. With appliqué, you are layering two layers of fabric, if not more. To keep the motifs dimensional, I press the appliquéd blocks on a folded hand towel. Turn the block upside down so the appliquéd shape is facing the towel and press. The towel gives a soft area for the shape to nestle in, so it stays dimensional and does not get flat or crushed.

In contrast to appliqué, when pressing pieced units (like the background square for the **Rail Fence with Stars** quilt), use a firm pressing surface. Press the seam allowances the direction the arrows indicate in the instructions. When pressing the seams in one direction always press the pieced block from the right side of the fabric; this helps avoid pressing in little tucks.

Pinning

Appliqué

When appliquéing, you need to pin the shapes into place onto the background fabric. If you are using the longer silk pins and find that they are getting in the way of your thread, pin from the wrong side of the block. This will help prevent the thread from getting tangled in the pins.

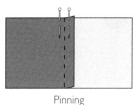

Pinning

Piecing

For aligning seams that have been pressed in opposite directions, place a pin no more than ⅛" on each side of the seam.

Sets

A set refers to the way the blocks are laid out and sewn before the borders are attached. There are two different types of sets used in this book. In a straight set the blocks are positioned with the sides parallel to the edge of the quilt. In a diagonal set, the blocks are sewn on point and sewn in rows across the diagonal.

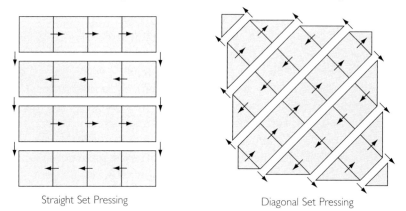

Straight Set Pressing   Diagonal Set Pressing

In both cases, once the blocks are sewn into rows, it is best to press each row in alternating directions (row 1 right, row 2 left, and so on). This will help you easily align the seams when sewing the rows together. After sewing the rows together, press the seams in one direction.

Borders

If you precut your borders, always add a few extra inches to the length. To determine the exact length of the border strips, measure your sewn quilt top across the center from top to bottom and from side to side. Compare your measurements to the project instructions and, if necessary, adjust the cutting measurements of the border strips to the actual length and width of your quilt top.

Appliquéd Borders

There are two methods to choose from if the borders are to be appliquéd.

Method One: You can attach the borders to the quilt top and then stitch the appliqué motifs. If this is your first attempt at appliquéing a border and if your project is small, this method is easier than Method Two for stitching the corner sections of the appliqué.

Method Two: Some quilters feel that borders should be appliquéd before attaching them to the quilt top. This is especially true if the project is large since the large quilt top can be cumbersome to manage, and there can be some distortion and shrinkage of the border length through the appliqué process. You should allow for this shrinkage by cutting the border strips a little longer than will be needed for the finished border length. Then trim them to the correct length after the appliqué is complete. For this method, if the border has a shape that turns the corner, leave enough appliqué to complete the corner once the border is sewn onto the quilt top. Notice on **Rose Sampler**, page 39, how the flower covers the joining of the vine sections.

10

Finishing

Backing

Once you have finished your quilt top, it is time to consider your backing. Always use 100% cotton fabric of the same quality as your appliquéd quilt top. If your project is larger than 42", it will be necessary to piece the backing. It is all right to use different fabrics for the pieced backing. My only caution is that if the quilt top has a light background, like the *Rose Sampler* quilt, be sure to use a light-colored backing. If you use a brightly colored piece of cloth for the backing, the color will show through to the top, which detracts from the finished look of the quilt. When preparing your backing, keep these rules in mind.

- Never use a sheet or decorator fabric. The thread count is very dense and is difficult to hand quilt through.
- Always cut off the selvage edges before piecing the backing fabric together; the seam might not lie flat and the selvage is difficult to hand quilt through.
- Prewash your background fabric and always cut it at least 2" larger on all sides of the quilt top. This allows for any shifting that might occur during quilting.

Batting

For hand quilting, I recommend starting with a low-loft, polyester batting. It makes quilting much easier.

For machine quilting, I recommend that you use 100% cotton batting. Please read the instructions on the batting package before using; some brands have prewashing instructions.

Layering

Place the backing wrong side up on a non-scratchable table top or on a non-loop carpet. The backing can be taped down (table top) or pinned using T-pins (carpet). Carefully smooth the batting onto the backing. Trim the batting to the same size as the backing. Smooth the quilt top over the batting, right side up. Pin the edges of the quilt top to keep it taut and prevent shifting.

Basting

For hand quilting, use a large needle and a neutral-colored thread. Baste in approximately a 4" grid so there is an equal amount of basting over the entire quilt surface. Never skimp on this process, as your quilt may slip and move during the quilting process.

For machine quilting, unlike hand quilting, pin-baste every 3" with small safety pins (brass pins are easiest to use). The pins should be no more than 3" apart and distributed evenly over the entire surface, avoiding areas where you will be stitching.

Quilting

I love hand quilting and think it is especially appropriate for hand appliqué; however, time does not always allow for this. For either hand quilting or machine quilting on appliqué, I have a few thoughts to share with you.

- More is better—never shortchange your quilt in the quilting process.
- Consider quilting in-the-ditch around the appliquéd shapes to hold them down.
- It's OK to quilt over the appliquéd units, either to continue a pattern or to accentuate details of the appliquéd shape.
- Use an equal amount of quilting over the entire surface. If you quilt different areas with unequal density your quilt will not only look odd, but will also not lie or hang nicely.

Binding

The final step in constructing a quilt is the binding.

1. Trim the backing and batting even with the edges of the quilt top.
2. Cut 2⅛" binding strips (or a little wider if you prefer). If necessary, piece the strips together using a diagonal seam, trim, and press open.
3. Trim two of the strips the width of the quilt plus 1". Fold and press lengthwise.

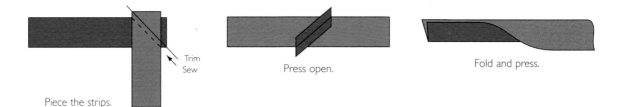

Trim
Sew

Press open.

Fold and press.

Piece the strips.

4. On the top edge of the quilt, align the raw edges of the binding with the raw edges of the quilt. Let the binding extend ½" past the corners of the quilt. Pin and then sew using a ¼" seam allowance. Repeat on the bottom edge of the quilt.
5. Bring the folded edge of the binding over the raw edges of the quilt and slip-stitch to the back of the quilt. Trim the ends even with the edge of the quilt.
6. For the two sides of the quilt, cut the binding the length of the quilt plus ½" for turning under. Fold the two ends of the binding to create a finished edge, and stitch. Again, turn the folded edge of the binding over the raw edge of the quilt and slip stitch into place.

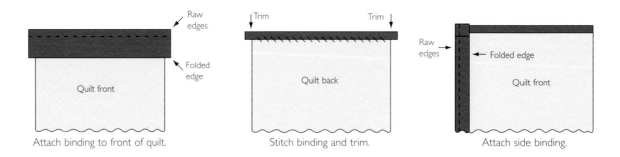

Raw edges

Folded edge

Quilt front

Attach binding to front of quilt.

Trim   Trim

Quilt back

Stitch binding and trim.

Raw edges → ← Folded edge

Quilt front

Attach side binding.

With the addition of a label that documents the date and name of the quiltmaker along with any interesting stories that pertain to your quilt, your project is complete.

Basic Appliqué Preparation

Let's get started! Appliqué is not an exact science. There are several ways to achieve the end product. Here are some different techniques to prepare your fabric shape for appliqué to achieve a beautiful result. Try them all and decide which works best for you. Keep in mind that different preparations will be appropriate for different shapes.

Right side   Wrong side

Thread Basting on Paper

Although this appliqué preparation method is the most time consuming of the methods presented here, I still use this technique when working with more complicated shapes. It gives me the confidence that the appliquéd piece will look like the original pattern.

Create several templates out of freezer paper the exact size of the shape you are going to appliqué. Every shape will require a paper template. To save time you can cut multiple, same-sized shapes of freezer paper by layering up to six pieces of freezer paper, glossy side down, and pressing them together. Cut the desired shape and peel the layers apart. Press the individual freezer-paper shapes, glossy side down, onto the WRONG side of the fabric. Carefully trim the fabric leaving ³⁄₁₆" seam allowance around the outside of the freezer-paper shape.

Knot one end of the thread, turn under the edge of the appliqué shape to the paper pattern, and baste through all three layers. Never use colored thread when basting—the dye might migrate onto the fabric. The success of the shape will be determined by the care taken when basting. Make sure all the edges look exactly how you want the finished shape to look.

After the shape is appliquéd, remove the basting stitches, slit the background fabric under the shape, and remove the paper.

Glue-Stick Basting on Paper

Using a glue stick minimizes the amount of preparation time by taking the place of basting with thread. The problem is that the glue is sticky, and can prevent the needle from gliding easily through the layers of cloth when appliquéing. However, some people really like this technique and find that this inconvenience is worth the time saved by not having to baste. Give it a try; you might like it.

Create several templates out of freezer paper the exact size of the shape you are going to appliqué. Every shape will require a paper template. As with thread basting, to save time, you can cut multiple, same-sized shapes of freezer paper by layering up to six pieces of freezer paper, glossy side down, and pressing. Cut the desired shape and peel the layers apart. Press the individual freezer-paper shapes, glossy side down, onto the WRONG side of the fabric. Carefully trim the fabric $3/16"$ around the outside freezer-paper shape.

Carefully rub the glue stick $1/8"$ around the outside edge of the paper shape. Rub the glue stick around the outside edge of the wrong side of the fabric. Carefully manipulating the fabric, fold the $3/16"$ seam allowance over the edge of the paper and pinch it into place with your fingers, or try using an orange stick or toothpick. To prevent your needle from getting sticky, avoid getting the glue on the fabric where the needle will be passing through.

Drawn Line for Needle-Turn Appliqué

This is my favorite way to work with simple shapes. The drawn line gives me the confidence to achieve the desired shape and little preparation is needed.

Create the shape out of template plastic or cardboard. Do not add a $3/16"$ seam allowance to the template. Place the template on the right side of the fabric and trace around the shape with a non-permanent marker. Carefully trim the fabric a scant $3/16"$ around the outside drawn line. The piece is ready to appliqué.

Preparation for Reverse Appliqué

Reverse appliqué is great for rounded shapes or shapes that you want to recede—like eyes on a cat. It really isn't difficult, it is just the reverse of traditional appliqué, thus the name. Rather than appliquéing a piece of fabric on top of another piece, with reverse appliqué, you layer the fabrics and cut away the top piece of fabric to reveal the fabric below.

Create the shape out of template plastic or cardboard. Do not add a $3/16"$ seam allowance to the template. Place the template on the right side of the top piece of fabric and trace around the shape with a non-permanent marker. Trim $3/16"$ on the inside of the shape. Layer the top fabric on top of the piece you want to reveal and pin together.

Preparation for Buttonhole Stitch

Another fun appliqué technique to try is buttonhole stitch.

Note: *When using the following method, keep in mind that the finished shape will be the mirror image of the original traced shape.*

For a shape that will be repeated, cut the shape out of template plastic or cardboard. Trace the shape on the paper side of the lightweight fusible adhesive. (It is very important to use lightweight fusible web when hand stitching.) Cut the shape out of the fusible web, adding about ¼" extra on all sides. Follow the pressing instructions on the fusible web, and press the fusible side down onto the wrong side of the fabric. Trim the bonded fusible shape to the exact size of the motif. Peel off the paper backing of the fusible web and iron onto the background fabric. The stitches will cover the raw edges.

Arrangement of Appliqué Pieces

All the patterns in this book are fairly simple and easy to arrange on the background pieces. I fold the background fabric to find the center, and then arrange the pieces accordingly.

As your love of appliqué grows and you progress to more difficult patterns it will become necessary to mark the background fabric for appliqué shape placement. Simply pin the pattern, right side up, onto the wrong side of the background fabric. Using a light box or window, lightly trace the placement of the shapes onto the fabric with a non-permanent marking tool. Be careful to be very light-handed with your marking tool, as it is often difficult to match the appliquéd shape exactly to the area where it will be placed.

Preparation for the Appliqué Stitch

Thread your needle with the thread still on the spool. Tie a single knot about 18 inches down the length of the thread (never any longer, to avoid tangling), and then snip off the thread from the spool. This will keep the "wrap" of the thread going in the right direction, resulting in less tangling.

Now it's time to stitch.

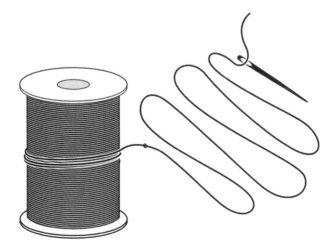

The Appliqué Stitch

The appliqué stitch is quite simple. Typically, if you are right-handed, you will stitch right to left (or counter-clockwise). Lefties usually stitch from left side to right (or clockwise).

The Basic Appliqué Stitch directions below are for appliqué shapes prepared for needle-turn (page 14) appliqué. For basted shapes (page 13) follow the instructions below, but keep in mind that you have already basted the edges of the shape under. The appliqué stitch is the same for both methods.

The Basic Appliqué Stitch

Left-handed   **Right-handed**

1. The best place to start is on a straight or slightly rounded edge. Fold under the edge of the shape, on the marked line, where you will begin stitching. From the back of the shape, come through the fabric exactly at the folded edge you want to appliqué. The knot will hide on the back of the fabric. Use the tip of the needle to turn the fabric edge under to create the fold on which you will continue stitching. Turn under only the amount of fabric you can stitch at one time (about 1/2").

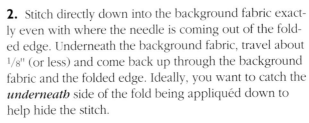 

2. Stitch directly down into the background fabric exactly even with where the needle is coming out of the folded edge. Underneath the background fabric, travel about 1/8" (or less) and come back up through the background fabric and the folded edge. Ideally, you want to catch the *underneath* side of the fold being appliquéd down to help hide the stitch.

3. Continue by stitching as you did in Step 2. Always pull the thread just taut enough—not too tight, not too loose.

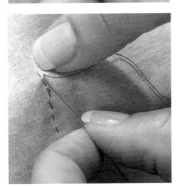 

4. When you finish stitching the appliqué shape, insert the needle directly down into the background fabric and pull the needle from the wrong side to make the thread taut. On the wrong side of the appliqué piece, take a minute stitch under the appliqué piece near the last stitch.

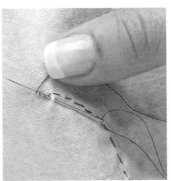

5. Wrap the thread around the needle twice and pull the thread through. Cut off the thread.

Outside Curves

Typically, curves can be maneuvered using the bias as your friend. If you cut out the appliqué shape with the curve on the bias of the fabric, the curved edge will be much easier to appliqué. However, if the shape you are working on has a very tight curve, consider paper basting first.

HINT: *If you have difficulty turning under the fabric edge, try using a wooden toothpick. The wood grabs the fabric, making it easier to turn under.*

Inside Curves

Left-handed   **Right-handed**

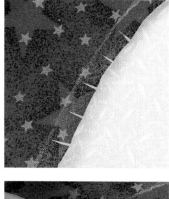

1. As you approach the inside curve, use very sharp scissors to clip just to the marked line—the tighter the curve, the more times you will need to clip.

2. Use the needle to turn under the edge of the appliqué shape to the marked line. Careful turning will achieve a smooth curve. Use basic appliqué stitches (page 16) very close together to appliqué the curve.

V's (inside angles)

1. As you approach the "V" shape use very sharp scissors and cut directly toward the center of the "V" all the way to the marked line.

2. Continue the basic appliqué stitch until you get to the "V." Be sure to turn the raw edge under a few threads at the "V." Take the stitch that will hold the inside corner in place. Make another stitch in the same place. This will keep the inset cut from fraying.

3. Continue to turn under the seam allowance and stitch.

Points

Points come in all shapes and sizes. The sharper the point the more finesse it will take to create a perfect point.

1. Trim the seam allowance (turn under) to $3/16''$. Stitch toward the point, turning the seam allowance under as you stitch.

2. Continue to stitch, bringing the needle up at the tip of the marked point.

3. Take a stitch at the very tip of the point. Carefully trim away some of the excess seam allowance fabric underneath the appliquéd shape at the end of the point that was just stitched. The sharper the point, the smaller the seam allowance should be.

4. Using the tip of your needle, gently tuck in the raw edge of the other side of the point. It will take two passes. Anchor the tip of the point one more time with another stitch. Pull the thread taut to help define the appliqué point. For paper-basted shapes, simply baste the points in place, trimming the seam allowance so the tip looks sharp and clean.

5. Continue to turn under the seam allowance and stitch.

Circles

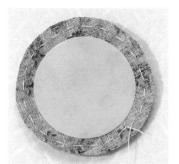

1. Cut the circle the desired finished size out of a heat resistant template material (Templar). Make sure that the circle is perfect. There are some precut template circles available on the market. Put the circle template on your fabric and cut out the circle 3/16" larger all the way around. Knot the end of the thread. Take a back stitch and sew a running stitch around the edge of the fabric circle.

2. Pull the thread to gather the circle of fabric like a shower cap around the plastic template until taut. Smooth out any folds. With a very hot steam iron press the circle of fabric while it is still around the plastic shape. I apply spray starch and press it again for extra hold.

3. After the circle is pressed and completely dry, loosen the gathering thread and carefully remove the plastic template. Again, gently pull the thread taut to form a perfect circle. Some people like to use coins or washers instead of the plastic template, however because of the thickness of the metal it is harder to get a crisp, pressed edge.

4. Use the basic appliqué stitch to sew around the circle—clockwise for left-handed, counter-clockwise for right-handed.

Bias Strips Without Bias Bars

Left-handed

Right-handed

1. For a bias stem without using bias bars, cut a bias strip the width desired multiplied by two, and add 1/2". Fold in half along the length of the strip and press. Hand or machine stitch the strip 1/4" from the raw edge directly onto the background fabric.

2. Carefully press the folded edge over the seam line covering the seam allowance. Stitch using the basic appliqué stitch (page 16). If your stem is less than 1/4" wide and the folded edge doesn't cover the raw edge, trim the excess seam allowance.

Bias Strips With Bias Bars

To make a multiple-strip bias strip, follow Step 2 on page 12 for binding in order to piece the bias strips into the length needed.

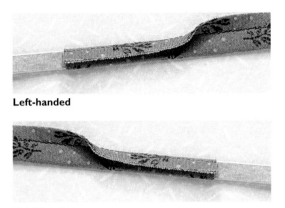

Left-handed

Right-handed

Cut a bias fabric strip the width of the bias bar multiplied by two, then add $1/2"$. With wrong sides together, fold in half along the length of the strip and press. Carefully sew using a $1/4"$ seam allowance. Insert the bar and gently roll the sewn seam to the underneath side. Trim the seam allowance if it protrudes beyond the finished edges of the bias strip. If you are using a multiple-strip bias strip, be sure the bias bar is inserted in the direction the seam allowances are pressed, so you will not be fighting against the seam allowances. Press. As each section is pressed (I like steam), move the bias bar down the tube and press again. CAUTION: The metal bars get very hot!

Buttonhole Stitch Appliqué

Buttonhole stitch is a lot of fun and worth exploring. One great thing about buttonhole stitch is that controlling the edges of the shape is easy because all shapes are cut exactly to size. I use this technique when I want a more casual look.

Left-handed

Right-handed

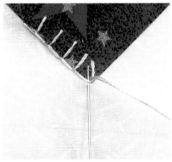

1. Bring the needle with the knotted thread up through the edge of the appliqué fabric. Hold the thread down with your thumb and go down through the appliqué fabric, then back up to make the stitch.

2. When you turn a corner, make an anchor stitch to hold the corner stitch.

Multi-Layered Appliqué

When preparing a shape that will have many layers, like the flowers on *Rose Sampler* (page 39), or the reversed appliquéd heart on the Samplers, it is a good idea to stitch the different layers together before they are sewn onto the quilt top. When appliquéing, it is easier to handle small pieces in this way, rather than trying to stitch them to the larger quilt background.

Once your appliquéd piece is finished, now comes the question of whether to cut away the background fabric behind the sewn shapes. If the piece is small and only one layer deep, like the small leaves on the samplers, I tend not to bother. However, if the shape is multi-layered like the flowers on *Rose Sampler*, it is worth taking the time to cut away all the layers. When it is time to hand quilt, you will be very sorry if there are multiple layers to contend with.

Color Sampler

Size: 28½" x 30½". Hand appliquéd and machine pieced by Alex Anderson. Machine quilted by Paula Reid.

This is an excellent project for experimenting with all of the different types of appliqué. I used reverse appliqué for the heart, needle-turn for the leaves, paper basting for the flowers and stars, bias bars for the outer border vine, and stitch-and-flip for the stems in the vase.

Fabric Tips

Picking fabric for these two samplers (pages 21 and 25) was fun—each quilt resulted in a very different look. The traditional look was created by using Thimbleberries™ fabrics by RJR Fashion Fabrics. The brighter sampler was created using fabrics from my collection to achieve a crisp, clean look. However you choose to work, experiment and play with your fabrics until the picture sampler reflects you!

Fabric Requirements

Yardage is based on a 42" fabric width. The following instructions give the total yardage needed to complete your quilt.

Light-colored Prints:	1 yard total for the background rectangles and the outer border
Bright Prints:	¾ yard total for the appliqué motifs and the pieced inner border
Green Scraps:	⅝ yard total for the leaves, stems, and vine
Backing:	1 yard
Coordinating Print:	⅜ yard for binding
Batting:	32" x 34"

22

Cutting

Light-colored Print

- Cut one strip 4½" x 42" for the top and bottom outer borders. Cut in half (4½" x 21").
- Cut 2 strips, 4½" x 42" for the side outer borders.
- Cut one rectangle 8" x 11" (A) for the appliqué background.
- Cut one square 11" x 11" (B) for the appliqué background.
- Cut one rectangle 6" x 18½" (C) for the appliqué background.

Bright Prints

- Cut one using the vase template pattern.
- Cut one square 4" x 4" for the reverse appliqué heart.
- Cut 38 squares 2½" x 2½" for the pieced inner border.
- Cut 3 using the flower template pattern.
- Cut 48 using the circle template pattern. Three of these will be used for flower centers.
- Cut 3 using the star template pattern.

Green Scraps

- Cut 28 using the leaf template pattern.
- Cut 1"-wide bias strips. Piece together for a total of 130" for the stems and vine.

Background Construction

Arrows indicate pressing direction.

1. Stitch Rectangle A to Rectangle B along the 11" sides. Press seam open.
2. Add Rectangle C. Press seam open. The background will measure 16½" x 18½".

Appliqué

1. Trace the heart onto the right side of the vase fabric. Use the 4" x 4" square for the heart. See page 14 for reverse appliqué instructions.
2. Prepare the appliqué pieces, bias stems, and vine following the instructions for your preferred method beginning on pages 13 and 19.
3. Appliqué the pieces to the background following the instructions for your preferred method beginning on page 16. I appliquéd the shapes in this order: stems, vase, flowers, stars.
4. Press from the back (page 9).

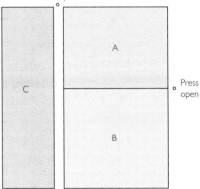

Press open

Press open

Stitch A to B, then add C.

Add Borders.

Borders

Arrows indicate pressing direction. Use ¼" seam allowance.

Pieced Inner Border

1. Make two borders of 8 bright-colored squares. Press seams in one direction.

2. Sew these borders to the top and bottom of the quilt top. Press seams toward the quilt top.

3. Make two borders of 11 bright-colored squares. Press seams in one direction.

4. Sew these borders to the sides of the quilt top. Press seams toward the quilt top.

5. Your quilt top should measure 20½" x 22½". If it does, use the following instructions to trim and attach the borders. If it doesn't, see page 10 to measure and cut the correct border lengths for your quilt top.

Appliquéd Outer Border

1. Trim two of the outer border strips to 20½" long and attach them to the top and bottom of the quilt top. Press the seams toward the outer borders.

2. Trim the two remaining outer border strips to 30½" long and attach to the sides of the quilt top. Press the seams toward the outer borders.

3. Press the border strips in half widthwise and lengthwise to find the midpoint. Arrange and pin the bias vine to the outer borders in a smooth curve that is pleasing to you. Appliqué following the instructions for your preferred method, beginning on page 19.

4. Arrange and pin the leaves and berries as desired along the vine. Stitch the appliqué pieces to the outer border. Press from the back (page 9).

Finishing

Layer, baste, quilt, bind, and label following the instructions beginning on page 11.

24

Country Sampler, 28½" × 30½". *Color Sampler* using an alternate color scheme
Hand appliquéd by Nancy Sands. Machine pieced by Alex Anderson.
Machine quilted by Paula Reid.

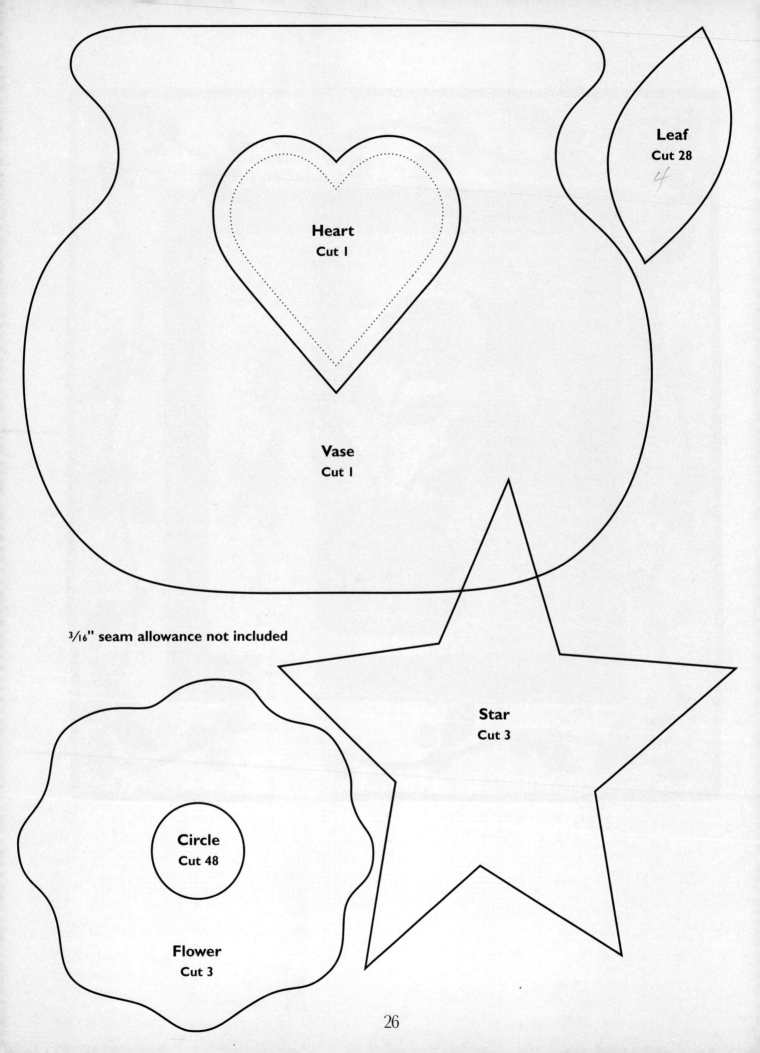

Leaf
Cut 28

Heart
Cut 1

Vase
Cut 1

³/₁₆" seam allowance not included

Star
Cut 3

Circle
Cut 48

Flower
Cut 3

26

Autumn Leaves

Size: 47½" x 47½". Hand appliquéd by Alex Anderson and Nancy Sands. Machine pieced by Alex Anderson. Machine quilted by Paula Reid.

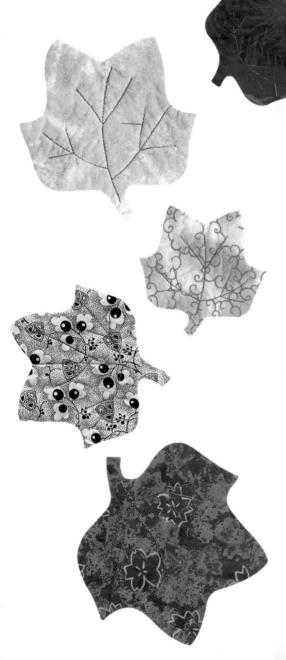

The leaf shape is fairly simple and can be appliquéd using the paper-basting method or needle-turn appliqué. The slightly rounded tips and gentle curves of the leaf make this quilt a perfect first project.

Fabric Tips

The mood of this quilt was inspired by the interesting border fabric. Notice how the color choices for the leaves bridged into the pink family. The varied black background fabrics give the quilt a lot of movement; much like blowing leaves on a cool fall day.

Fabric Requirements

Yardage is based on a 42" fabric width. The following instructions give the total yardage needed to complete the quilt.

Dark-colored Prints:	1½ yards total for the background squares and setting triangles
Bright- and Light-colored Prints:	1 yard total for the leaves
Stripe:	¼ yard for the inner border
Large-scale Print:	1⅜ yards for the outer border
Backing:	2⅞ yards
Black Print:	⅜ yard for binding
Batting:	51" x 51"

Cutting

Dark-colored Prints

- Cut 25 squares 7½" x 7½". (These squares will be trimmed after the appliqué is complete.)
- Cut one strip 9¾" x 42"; cut into 3 squares 9¾" x 9¾" . Cut each square in quarters diagonally for the side setting triangles. ⊠
- From the remainder of the 9¾" strip, cut into 2 squares 5⅛" x 5⅛". Cut each square in half diagonally for the corner setting triangles. ◻

Note: Put the side and corner setting triangles in a resealable bag to prevent the bias edges from stretching until you use them.

Bright- and Light-colored Prints

- Cut 25 using the leaf template pattern.

Stripe

- Cut 4 strips 1½" x 42" for the inner borders.

Large-scale Print

- Cut 4 lengthwise strips 6" x the fabric length for the top and bottom outer borders.

Appliqué

I. Prepare the appliqué leaves following the instructions for your preferred method beginning on page 13.

2. Appliqué the leaves to the background squares following the instructions for your preferred method beginning on page 16.

3. Press the blocks from the back (page 9).

4. Trim each block to measure 6½" x 6½".

Quilt Top Assembly

Arrows indicate pressing direction. Use ¼" seam allowance.

I. Stitch the blocks into diagonal rows, adding corner and side triangles. Press the seams of each row in opposite directions.

2. Stitch the rows together. Press.

3. Your quilt top should measure 34½" x 34½". If it does, use the instructions below to trim and attach the borders. If it doesn't, see page 10 to measure and cut the correct border lengths for your quilt top.

Borders

I. Trim two of the inner border strips to 34½" long and attach them to the top and bottom of the quilt top. Press the seams toward the borders.

2. Trim the two remaining inner border strips to 36½" long and attach to the sides of the quilt top. Press the seams toward the borders.

3. Trim two of the outer border strips to 36½" long and attach them to the top and bottom of the quilt top. Press the seams toward the inner borders.

4. Trim the two remaining outer border strips to 47½" long and attach to the sides of the quilt top. Press the seams toward the inner borders.

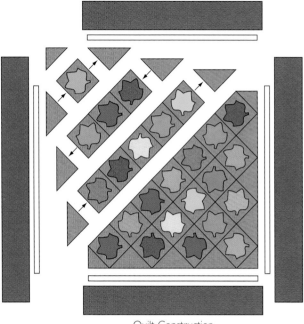

Quilt Construction

Finishing

Layer, baste, quilt, bind, and label following the instructions beginning on page 11.

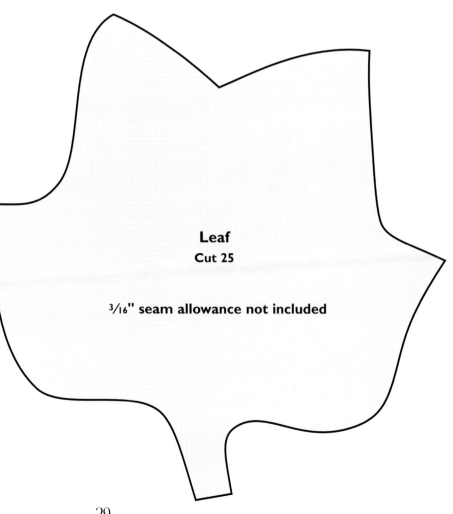

Leaf

Cut 25

³⁄₁₆" seam allowance not included

Cherries

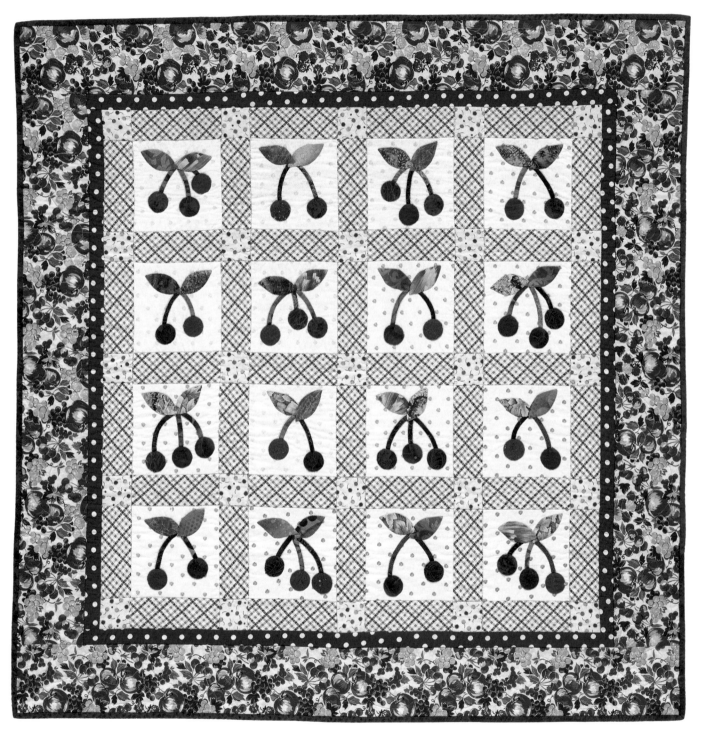

Size: 45" x 45". Hand appliquéd and machine pieced by Alex Anderson. Machine quilted by Paula Reid.

This quilt is really quite simple, but it uses three different appliqué techniques: bias stems, circles, and simple leaves. This would be another strong candidate for a first appliqué project.

Fabric Tips

The colors for this quilt were dictated entirely by the great '40s reproduction fabric used for the border. Several different greens and reds were used to create the look of actual cherries and leaves. The feeling of this quilt reminds me of hot summer days in times gone by.

Fabric Requirements

Yardage is based on a 42" fabric width. The following instructions give the total yardage needed to complete the quilt.

Light-colored Prints:	1⅛ yards total for the background squares
Red Scraps:	¼ yard total for the cherries
Green Scraps:	¾ yard total for the leaves and stems
Print:	⅝ yard for sashing
Print:	¼ yard for the sashing posts
Blue-and-white Polka Dot:	¼ yard for inner border
'40s Print:	1⅜ yards for outer border
Backing:	2¾ yards
Red Print:	⅜ yard for the binding
Batting:	49" x 49"

Cutting

Light-colored Prints

- Cut 16 squares 7½" x 7½" for the background squares. (These squares will be trimmed after the appliqué is complete.)

Red Scraps

- Cut 40 using the cherry template pattern.

Green Scraps

- Cut 32 using the leaf template pattern.
- Cut approximately 160" of 1"-wide bias strips for the stems.

Prints for Sashing and Posts

- Cut 7 strips 2½" x 42"; cut into 40 rectangles 2½" x 6½" for the sashing.
- Cut 2 strips 2½" x 42"; cut into 25 squares 2½" x 2½" for the sashing posts.

Polka Dot

- Cut 4 strips 1½" x 42" for the inner borders.

'40s Print

- Cut 4 strips 5" x the fabric length for the outer borders.

Appliqué

1. Prepare the appliqué pieces following the instructions for your preferred method beginning on page 13.

2. Appliqué the pieces to the background squares following the instructions for your preferred method beginning on page 16.

3. Press the blocks from the back (page 9).

4. Trim each block to measure 6½" x 6½".

Quilt Top Assembly

Arrows indicate pressing direction. Use ¼" seam allowance.

1. Stitch the blocks into four rows adding the short sashing strips between the blocks. Press the seams toward the sashing.

2. Make five rows of sashing and posts. Press the seams toward the sashing.

3. Alternate sashing/post and block/sashing rows and stitch the rows together. Press.

4. Your quilt top should measure 34 ½" x 34½". If it does, use the instructions below to trim and attach the borders. If it doesn't, see page 10 to measure and cut the correct border lengths for your quilt top.

Borders

1. Trim two of the inner border strips to 34½" long and attach them to the sides of the quilt top. Press the seams toward the borders.

2. Trim the two remaining inner border strips to 36½" long and attach to the top and bottom of the quilt top. Press the seams toward the borders.

3. Trim two of the outer border strips to 36½" long and attach them to the sides of the quilt top. Press the seams toward the inner borders.

4. Trim the two remaining outer border strips to 45½" long and attach to the top and bottom of the quilt top. Press the seams toward the inner borders.

Finishing

Layer, baste, quilt, bind, and label following the instructions beginning on page 11.

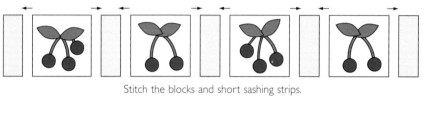

Stitch the blocks and short sashing strips.

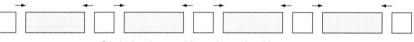

Stitch the short sashing strips and sashing posts.

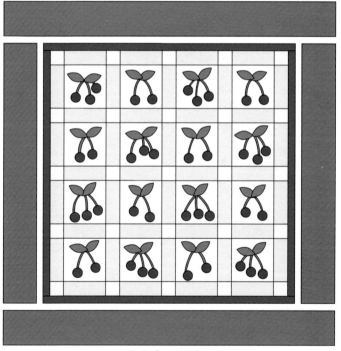

Quilt Construction

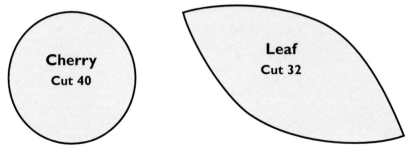

Cherry Cut 40

Leaf Cut 32

³⁄₁₆" seam allowance not included

32

Hearts

Size: 50¼" × 50¼". Hand appliquéd and pieced by Alex Anderson. Machine quilted by Paula Reid.

Everyone loves hearts and many people find them to be a perfect first appliqué project. Try using needle-turn or paper basting, both techniques work quite well with hearts.

Fabric Tips

Hearts are a reminder of hearth and home. To evoke this feeling, I chose to work with a delicious assortment of reproduction prints. Notice that different background fabrics have been used. The variety of fabrics give this quilt a fresh new look, with a historical touch.

Fabric Requirements

Yardage is based on a 42" fabric width. The following instructions give the total yardage needed to complete the quilt.

Light-colored Prints:	2 yards total for the background squares
Medium- and Dark-colored Prints:	1 yard total for the appliquéd hearts
Large-scale Print:	1½ yards for the setting and corner triangles and outer border
Dark tone-on-tone Print:	¼ yard for the inner border
Backing:	3⅛ yards
Green:	½ yard for the binding
Batting:	55" x 55"

Cutting

Light-colored Prints

- Cut 61 squares 6" x 6" for the background. (These squares will be trimmed after the appliqué is complete.)

Medium- and Dark-colored Prints

- Cut 61 hearts using the heart template pattern.

Large-scale Print

- Cut 4 lengthwise strips 5¾" x the fabric length for the outer borders.
- From the remaining fabric, cut 5 squares 7⅝" x 7⅝". Cut each square into quarters diagonally for the side setting triangles. ⊠
- Cut 2 squares 4" x 4" from the remaining fabric. Cut each square in half diagonally for the corner setting triangles. ◻

Note: Put the side and corner setting triangles in a resealable bag to prevent the bias edges from stretching until you use them.

Dark Tone-on-tone Print

- Cut 4 strips 1½" x 42" for the inner borders.

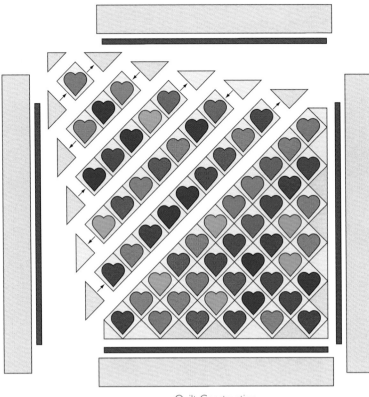

Quilt Construction

Appliqué

1. Prepare the appliqué hearts following the instructions for your preferred method beginning on page 13.

2. Appliqué the hearts to the background squares following the instructions for your preferred method beginning on page 16.

3. Press the blocks from the back (page 9).

4. Trim each block to measure 5" x 5".

Quilt Top Assembly

Arrows indicate pressing direction. Use ¼" seam allowance.

1. Stitch the blocks into diagonal rows adding corner and side triangles. Press the seams of each row in opposite directions.

2. Stitch the rows together. Press.

3. Your quilt top should measure 38¾" x 38¾". If it does, use the following instructions to trim and attach the borders. If it doesn't, see page 10 to measure and cut the correct border lengths for your quilt top.

Borders

1. Trim two of the inner border strips to 38¾" long and attach them to the top and bottom of the quilt top. Press the seams toward the borders.

2. Trim the two remaining inner border strips to 40¾" long and attach to the sides of the quilt top. Press the seams toward the borders.

3. Trim two of the outer border strips to 40¾" long and attach them to the top and bottom of the quilt top. Press the seams toward the inner borders.

4. Trim the two remaining outer border strips to 51¼" long and attach to the sides of the quilt top. Press the seams toward the inner borders.

Finishing

Layer, baste, quilt, bind, and label your quilt following the instructions beginning on page 11.

Heart
Cut 61

³⁄₁₆" seam allowance not included

Rail Fence with Stars

Size: 42¹/₂" x 48¹/₂". Machine pieced by Alex Anderson. Hand appliquéd by Alex Anderson and Nancy Sands. Machine quilted by Paula Reid.

The star tips are a bit more difficult to appliqué than some of the other shapes in this book, making this project a little challenging. I would suggest paper basting or needle-turn for this project.

Fabric Tips

Once resistant to using plaids, I now find plaid quilts completely charming. It is important to include a variety of different sizes and scales of plaids. Notice that one non-plaid fabric has been used. It is a millennium print that was given to me by a friend. This quilt has a patriotic, country feel.

Fabric Requirements

Yardage is based on a 42" fabric width. The following instructions give the total yardage needed to complete your quilt.

Beige Plaids:	⅛ yard each of fifteen different fabrics for the appliquéd Rail Fence block backgrounds
Blue-and-Red Plaids:	¼ yard each of five different fabrics for the border blocks and the appliquéd stars
Blue Plaids:	¼ yard each of five different fabrics for the border blocks and the appliquéd stars
Red Plaids:	¼ yard each of five different fabrics for the border blocks and the appliquéd stars
Backing:	2⅔ yards
Blue and Red Plaids:	⅓ yard total for binding
Batting:	46" x 52"

Cutting

Beige Plaids

■ Cut one 2½" x 42" strip from each for the appliqué Rail Fence block backgrounds.

Red, Blue, and Blue-and-Red Plaids

■ Cut one 2½" x 42" strip from each for the border blocks. Cut each strip in half lengthwise (2½" x 21").
■ Cut 30 stars using the star template pattern.

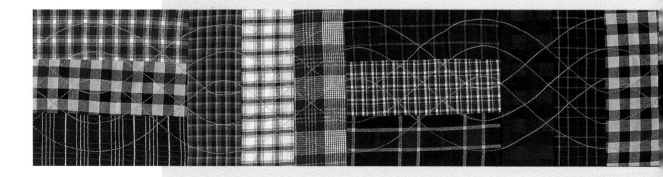

Block Assembly

1. Sew three beige plaid strips together along the long edges. Press. Repeat to make five strip set units.

6½"   6½"

Strip Set Units

2. Cut the strip sets into thirty 6½" x 6½" Rail Fence blocks.

Rail Fence Block

3. Repeat Step 1 using the red, blue, and blue-and-red plaids.

4. Cut the strip sets into twenty-six 6½" x 6½" Rail Fence blocks. Set aside until quilt assembly.

Appliqué

1. Prepare the appliqué stars following the instructions for your preferred method beginning on page 13.

2. Arrange the beige Rail Fence blocks referring to the quilt photograph (page 36). Pin the stars to the blocks exactly where you want them positioned.

3. Appliqué the stars to the beige Rail Fence blocks following the instructions for your preferred method beginning on page 16.

4. Press the blocks from the back (page 9).

Quilt Top Assembly

Arrows indicate pressing direction. Use ¼" seam allowance.

1. Arrange all the blocks referring to the quilt photograph.

2. Stitch the blocks into rows. Press.

3. Stitch the rows together. Press.

Finishing

Layer, baste, quilt, bind, and label your quilt following the instructions beginning on page 11.

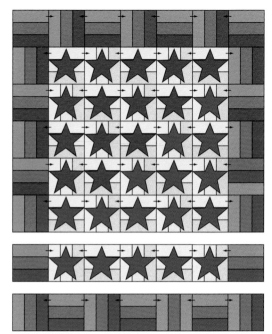

Note alternating directions of the Rail Fence blocks.

Star
Cut 30

³⁄₁₆" seam allowance not included

38

Rose Sampler

Size: 54½" x 54½". Hand appliquéd and machine pieced by Alex Anderson. Machine quilted by Paula Reid.

Fabric Tips

This quilt was put together without a lot of thought. I only wanted a bright and cheery look. Upon completion I realized that it looked like it came straight from Mexico, where I had been recently. It never ceases to amaze me where our inspirations come from.

Fabric Requirements

Yardage is based on a 42" fabric width. The following instructions give the total yardage needed to complete your quilt.

Off-white:	3 yards for the background squares, pieced inner border triangles, and appliqué border background
Yellow:	¼ yard for appliquéd flower and flower centers
Orange:	⅜ yard for appliquéd flowers and square-in-a-square border
Bright Pink:	½ yard for appliquéd flowers and square-in-a-square border
Red:	½ yard for appliquéd flowers, buds, and square-in-a-square border
Purple:	6" x 6"
Green Scraps:	1¼ yards total for leaves and buds
Green:	⅝ yard for stems and vine
Backing:	3¼ yards
Red:	½ yard for binding
Batting:	58" x 58"

Cutting

Off-white

- Cut 4 strips 9½" x 56" for the outer border background.
- Cut 4 squares 17" x 17" for the background blocks. (These squares will be trimmed after the appliqué is complete.)
- Cut 6 strips 2⅜" x 42"; cut into 88 squares 2⅜" x 2⅜". Cut each square in half diagonally for the pieced border. ◻

Note: Put the pieced border triangles in a resealable bag to prevent the bias edges from stretching until you use them.

Yellow

- Cut 52 using template pattern A; cut one using template pattern D.

Orange

- Cut one strip 2⅝" x 42" for the square-in-a-square border; cut into 15 squares 2⅝" x 2⅝".
- Cut 4 using template pattern B; cut 14 using template pattern C; cut 4 using template pattern G.

Bright Pink

- Cut one strip 2⅝" x 42"; cut into 16 squares 2⅝" x 2⅝" for the square-in-a-square border.
- Cut 8 using template pattern B; Cut 10 using template pattern C; cut one using template pattern D; cut 8 using template pattern G.

Red

- Cut one strip 2⅝" x 42"; cut into 13 squares 2⅝" x 2⅝" for the square-in-a-square border.
- Cut 6 from red using template pattern B; cut 12 using template pattern C; cut one using template pattern D; cut 4 using template pattern F; cut 3 using template G.

Purple

- Cut one using template pattern E.

Green Scraps

- Cut 15 using template pattern H; cut 132 using template pattern I.
- Cut approximately 350" total of 1"-wide bias strips for the stems and vine.

Appliqué

1. Press each background square in half vertically and horizontally. Open the square and lightly press it in half diagonally (from corner to corner) in both directions, being careful not to press out the horizontal and vertical creases. Use these pressed lines to center and position your applique pieces (page 42).

2. Prepare the appliqué pieces following the instructions for your preferred method beginning on page 13.

3. Appliqué the pieces to the background squares following the instructions for your preferred method beginning on page 16.

Position the large flower motif in the center of the block before positioning and stitching the stems in place. You will also need approximately 21" of bias stems from green scraps to make three 3½"-long stems and one 6½"-long stem.

Position the flower motif in the center of the block before positioning and stitching the stems in place. You will also need approximately 38" of bias stems from green scraps to make four 4½"-long straight stems and four 3¼"-long curved stems.

Position the flower motif in the center of the block before positioning and stitching the stems in place. You will also need approximately 30" of bias stems from green scraps to make eight 3"-long stems.

Position the flower motif in the center of the block before positioning and stitching the stems in place. You will also need approximately 30" of bias stems from green scraps to make four 1¾"-long stems and four 4"-long stems.

1. Press the blocks from the back (page 9).
2. Trim each block to measure 15½" x 15½".

Quilt Top Assembly

Use ¼" seam allowance.

1. Sew two blocks together. Press seam to one side.

2. Sew the remaining two blocks together and press the seam in the opposite direction as you did the seam between the first two blocks.

3. Stitch the four blocks together. Press.

Borders

SQUARE-IN-A-SQUARE BORDER

Arrows indicate pressing direction.

1. Sew two background triangles to the opposite sides of each square. Press seams toward the triangles.

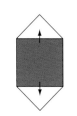

Sew triangles to opposite sides of each square.

2. Sew two background triangles to the remaining opposite sides of each square. Press seams toward the triangles.

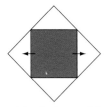

Sew triangles to remaining opposite sides of each square.

3. Arrange the square-in-a-square blocks as desired.

4. Make two borders of 10 blocks and two borders of 12 blocks. Press seams open.

Add Border

5. Sew the two borders of 10 blocks to the opposite sides of the quilt top. Be careful to match the seam of the square-in-a-square blocks with the seam between the appliqué blocks. Press seams toward appliqué blocks.

6. Sew the remaining borders of 12 blocks to the remaining sides of the quilt top. Be careful to match the seams in the corners as well as the seam of the square-in-a-square blocks with the seam between the appliqué blocks. Press seams toward the appliqué blocks.

APPLIQUÉ BORDER

HINT: *You will need approx-imately 200" of bias stems from green scraps to make the vine.*

1. Your quilt top should measure 36½" x 36½". If it does, use the following instructions to appliqué, trim, and attach the borders. If it doesn't, see page 10 to measure and cut the correct border lengths for your quilt top.

2. Press the border pieces in half vertically and horizontally. Use these creases as placement lines for the appliqué pieces. Use the photograph to help with the placement.

3. Appliqué the borders. Leave enough vine to turn the corner and cover where the stems join with a leaf or flower once the border is sewn onto the quilt top. Press from the back (page 9).

4. Trim two of the outer border strips to 36½" long and attach them to the top and bottom of the quilt top. Press the seams toward the borders.

5. Trim the two remaining outer border strips to 54½" long and attach to the sides of the quilt top. Press the seams toward the borders.

Finishing

Layer, baste, quilt, bind, and label following the instructions beginning on page 11.

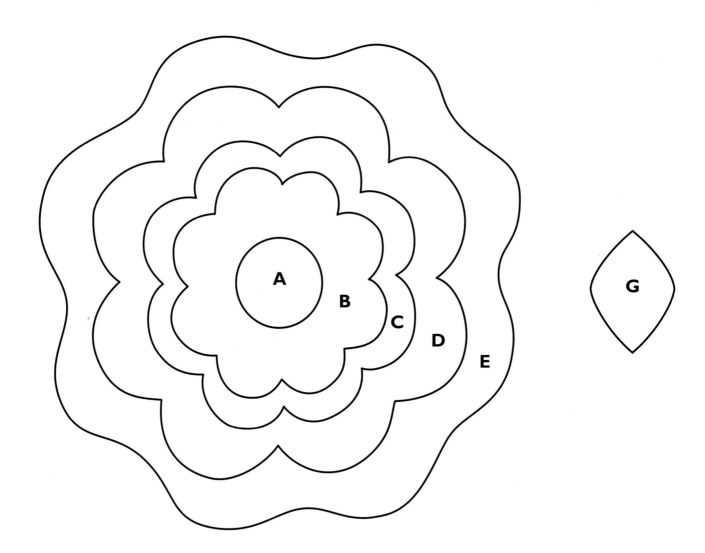

A

B

C

D

E

G

³⁄₁₆" seam allowance not included

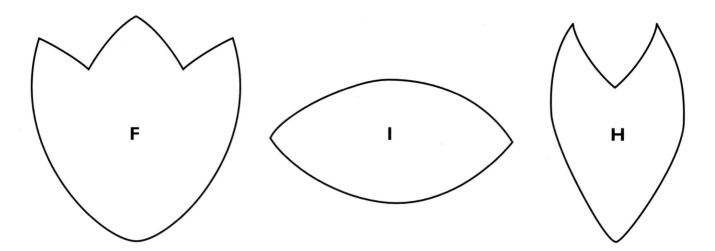

F

I

H

Mittens

Size: 42½" × 36½". Buttonhole stitched by Alex Anderson and Nancy Sands. Machine pieced by Alex Anderson. Machine quilted by Paula Reid.

Last but not least, no appliqué book would be complete without a buttonhole stitch project. Buttonhole is a quick and fun way to create an entirely different look. This quilt is a fun take-along project for people on the go.

Fabric Tips

This collection of Moda fabrics was given to me by Robyn Pandolph, the fabric designer. After designing the mitten pattern, I knew this fabric would be perfect. Notice how the embroidery floss color changes with each mitten, and adds another element to the quilt.

Fabric Requirements

Yardage is based on a 42" fabric width. The following instructions give the total yardage needed to complete the quilt.

Various Prints:	1 yard total for the background squares
Floral Prints:	1 yard total for the mittens
Light- to Medium-colored Prints:	⅞ yard total for the border
Backing:	1⅓ yards
Print:	⅓ yard for binding
Batting:	40" x 46"
Fusible Adhesive:	1¼ yards
Embroidery floss:	A variety of colors to complement the mittens

Cutting

Various Prints

■ Cut 5 rectangles 7½" x 13½" and 10 squares 7½" x 7½" for the background squares. (These pieces will be trimmed after the appliqué is complete.)

Floral Prints

■ Cut 20 using the mitten template pattern.

Light- to Medium-colored Prints

■ Cut 88 squares 3½" x 3½" for the border.

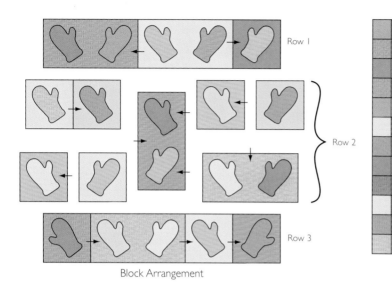

Row 1

Row 2

Row 3

Block Arrangement

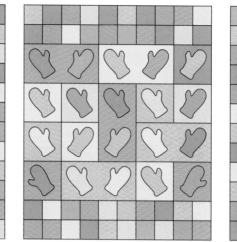
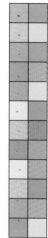

Quilt Construction

Appliqué

1. Prepare the mittens following the instructions for buttonhole stitch preparation beginning on page 15. Position the mittens on the background squares in an arrangement that is pleasing to you.

2. Buttonhole stitch the mittens to the background squares following the instructions beginning on page 20.

3. Press the blocks from the back (page 9).

4. Trim the rectangle blocks to measure 6½" x 12½" and the square blocks to measure 6½" x 6½".

Quilt Top Assembly

Arrows indicate pressing direction. Use ¼" seam allowance.

1. Arrange the blocks referring to the diagram and the quilt photograph.

2. Stitch the blocks into rows. Press the seams of each row in opposite directions.

3. Stitch the rows together. Press.

Borders

1. For the top border, stitch 10 of the 3½" squares together into one long row. Press the seams in one direction. Repeat. Stitch these two rows together along the long edges. Press. Repeat for the bottom borders.

2. For one side border, stitch 12 of the 3½" squares together into one long row. Press the seams in one direction. Repeat. Stitch these two rows together along the long edges. Press. Repeat for the other side border.

3. Sew the borders to the quilt top; first the top and bottom, then the sides. Press.

Finishing

Layer, baste, quilt, bind, and label your quilt following the instructions beginning on page 11.

Mitten
Trace 9 and trace 11 reversed on fusible adhesive.

About the Author

Alex Anderson's goal is to inspire and educate as many quilters as possible. Luckily, Alex is in a position to do just that. As host of HGTV's Simply Quilts, she is well-known to the quilting community. Her award-winning quilts have been displayed at shows around the country for more than twenty years, and widely published in books and magazines.

Alex describes her style of quiltmaking as "innovative-traditional." Her roots in the fine arts—she has a degree in art from San Francisco State University—and her deep appreciation for the work of quilters from past centuries have inspired her particular focus on fabric and color relationships along with traditional quilting designs.

Alex lives in northern California, with her family. Visit her website at alexandersonquilts.com.

Other books by Alex Anderson

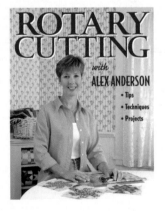 

For information about other C&T titles write for a free catalog:

C&T Publishing, Inc.
P.O. Box 1456
Lafayette, CA 94549
(800) 284-1114
e-mail: ctinfo@ctpub.com
website: www.ctpub.com

For quilting supplies:

Cotton Patch Mail Order
3405 Hall Lane, Dept. CTB
Lafayette, CA 94549
(800) 835-4418
(925) 283-7883
e-mail: quiltusa@yahoo.com
website: www.quiltusa.com